NEARLY IDENTICAL SHARKS

Julia Rose Lewis is [BIO HERE]

Also by Julia Rose Lewis

Postcards From Mental States [w/ Paul Hawkins]   (Hesterglock Press, 2023)

The Velvet Protocol [w/ Nathan Hyland Walker] (Knives Forks and Spoons, 2022)

High Erratic Ecology   (Knives Forks and Spoons Press, 2020)

The Hen Wife   (Contraband Books, 2020)

Miscellaneous   (Sampson Low, 2019)

NAG   (Gang Press, 2019)

How to Hypnotize a Lobster   (Fathom Books, 2018)

Archeology and the Beast   (Luminous Press, 2018)

Phenomenology of the Feral   (Knives Forks and Spoons Press, 2017)

Strays [w/ James Miller]   (HVTN Press 2017)

Exhalation Halves Lambda   (Finishing Line Press, 2017)

Zeroing Event   (Zarf Poetry, 2016)

Nearly Identical Sharks

Julia Rose Lewis

Broken Sleep Books

ISBN: 978-1-915760-20-3

Cover designed by Aaron Kent

Edited and typeset by Aaron Kent

Broken Sleep Books Ltd
Rhydwen
Talgarreg
Ceredigion
SA44 4HB

Broken Sleep Books Ltd
Fair View
St Georges Road
Cornwall
PL26 7YH

Contents

A witch ought never to be frightened in the darkest forest, Granny Weatherwax had once told her, because she should be sure in her soul that the most terrifying thing in the forest was her.

— Terry Pratchett, *Wintersmith*

Shall We Shellfish?

foolish mytilus
blue widely distributed
mussel trossulus
secretes the thread to bed down
hard substrates tonight
the gland is good night sleep tight

nitrogen singing
cytoxan and melphalan
must from mustard gas
pass from humans through mussels
what we eat we are
what we excrete into sound

The Hunting of the Shark

after the Emperor of All Maladies

one on and on and
on and on and on and on
and automaton

Sarcoma means to become fleshy from flesh. See neoplasm in the
common fowl for the tumor composed of soup of chicken insides
of cells insides of nucleuses. Between virus genes and normal genes
scientists found nearly no difference, then the scientists found
nearly identical sharks in sheep and geese cells. Scientists found
an oncogene, then the scientists found nearly identical sharks
in pheasants and turkeys cells. Then the scientists found nearly
identical sharks in ducks and cows cells. Then the scientists found
nearly identical sharks in newborn emu cells (because they were
only brave enough to biopsy a baby). Then the scientists found
nearly identical sharks in mice and quails cells. Then the scientists
found nearly identical sharks in fish and white rabbits cells. Then
the scientists found nearly identical sharks in human cells.

Oviparity

materialization
rough and leathery
and horns at the four corners
black collagen back
see through here through the egg case
cartilaginous
us of the rajiformes fish
no microscope no
bones inside the mermaid's purse
outline in the sun
eye the wrack line where high tide
deposits seaweed
here are rays near rays, near lay
identical sharks

Red Lizard

blind lizard's leg of
hell-broth boil and bubble
toil and trouble

If you give a witch an office of her own, she may hang her scaled reptiles above the door. Perhaps the lizards remind her of her commitment to ovoviviparity? To carry her young witches as far as she can. Her lizards are old. Their backs are brittle with little time left to gravity. She doesn't mind the blind reptiles, the legs lost to the door frame, the dry and faded tails. They regenerate bright blue, green, light blue, and red tails. The lizards are a part the dust on the bottoms of the young witches sitting and waiting at her door. Her dried reptiles remind her of true autonomy waiting in the laboratory. Standing under the lizards is the definition of liminal.

Silly Density

she eats peppermints
like a nightmare eats salt licks
flowers and lizards
my gift from the science gods
teeth keep themselves to themselves

Lab Examination

love her recipes
full of troubles, like a hell-
broth boils and bubbles

She teaches that it is chemicals, not turtles, all the way down.
"I make molecules productively during daytime" translates to:
Introduction, Main Reaction, Mechanism, Procedure with reference,
Diagrams of apparatus, Data and Observations. Her labor read her
story. She turned her body into a cauldron, toward collaboration.
The beauty of the hedgehog is the body of the problem; her research
embodies the problem. (Taxol is always the answer.) Paint thinner
or blood thinner, potion or poison, halogenated or non-halogenated
waste? Rats or mice or meese (because geese) made a mess of the
chocolates she left in our exam papers.

Meese

(green mice)

water pedestal
all founder domination
find invertebrate
the glacier oyster rolling
on cold dominion
the whole colony inside moss
from impurities
hybrid of pearls and tribbles
rolling rolling on
tracking macroscopic scales
trekking the arctic
birds or herd of wildebeests
fine-grained sediment
my gift from the science gods

Hippopotamouse

she is not a fool
if and only if a thief
a gray sieve driven
the river horse is sinking

riven habitat
exit in boiling water

hippopotamus
I will so hold your horses
herd to dale to bloat
little humpbacked horse ballet
it is informal
if fossil whales school themselves

PhD

no lidocaine gel
no razor clam to see here

after exercise
algae and eels and balloons
rest or rant or thin
the withers to the forelock

I will my fingers
no coral left unexplored

red and liver hair
follow flotsam and jetsam
aluminum comb
thinking to knot and shorten
if responsible
this nightmare in her fingers

Historical

or hysterical
is only a paper horse

gynecologist
on and on with the nightmare
rider or doctor
or gift from the science gods

tiger mare cares not
her ears are not bowling pins

Apollo's lady
an iron shovel lining
a jet velvet glove
is consent enshrined in forms

If Merrily

so we are ugly
bags of mostly salt water
if fair is farther
the billowing wins nine boats
woe is sail as white
guest on guest on guest nagging
as the protector
is the grey mare wassailing
winter ribbons bells
through and through mari lwyd

Failure to Villanelle

double double toil
and troubles dire spectrolite
and London puddles

I have to see a man about a theme, my gift from the arts gods. She
is my gift from the science gods, and a hedgehog. If you do not
believe that there are goods of the natural sciences, see hedgehogs,
not pigeons now, and never finches. This is not a hagiography of
the former, seriously the latter is smarter than that. All my poems
are love poems. Will the pigeons eat pineapple? I tell my gift from
the science gods that I would rather die of cancer than parkinson's
disease and she tells me I am right. I have so many names for
them. My gift from the arts gods: bear, clove oil, fighter, pear,
tree, phorophyte, the one with labradorite eyes. My gift from the
science gods: guardian angel, fighter, hedgehog, interpreter, toluene,
miracle, witch, the one with labradorite eyes. Remember that
the miracle of a bottle of diet cherry pepsi equals the miracle of
scrimshaw on a whale's tooth.

Guardian Angel

pebble pebble soil
and crumbles fire burns the round
bottom to bubbles

I remember counting out the glass vials of boiling stones, one for
every drawer. Here is still the drive to Berwyn; she is still alive.
The mile of stones through the hill of the king of the fairy folk
is american gods and guardian angels in reverse. Pass the upland
raptors including the hen harrier, merlin, and peregrine falcons on
the moorland wild with bracken and heather. What is this acidic
grassland where the short-eared owl thrives? The white crest of
Cadair Berwyn.

Moel Sych is called dry hill, recall the big hill of the seven sister
witches. Cadair Bronwen has a summit of white. When we meet
she says over and over that I look just the same, the same long
braid, as though the past decade hasn't come to pass.

Withers

Overflowing well
she was the bellwether hill
if life and winter
did grandmother all these storms,
the oyster river,
or yet frightening nurses.

The hag god nurses
tell the scientist draw well
the merry river
or yet lighting the big hill.
Inimical storms
ancestor horse and winter.

Nuclear winter
here to the unknown nurses
gallop mountain storms
piling the wool blankets well,
into a shawl hill.
The witch gives mist the river

nuclear river
neat is sugar in winter.
The galloping hill
scallops the hag god nurses.
Experiment well
through the muscle and the storms.

If following storms
devils or plastic river
is traveling well

through diminutive winter.
Protection nurses
the hospital means the hill.

To the pilgrim hill
she herds dear these mountain storms,
hormones, and nurses.
The hag god rushes the river
harvest in winter.
Well well well well well well well.

To be driven to the hill, the saline river
follows storms as the ferry wife fights in winter,
springing the nurses as clear or following well.

Shall We Shellfish?

here fertilizer
pollution levels pounds on
pounds of nitrogen
bring on the zooplankton
the blue-green blooming
confusion of phosphorous

the northwestern sound
sends us to deception pass
to swinomish pass
through the main basin drain the
body of water
we will follow the treatment

Future of Tattoos

trouble trouble oil
of cloves boiling it burns and
brings cauldron bubbles

Here is the hematology of tattoo ink. Pre-dispersed or pigments
made of rust, metal salts, and plastics plus water, sometimes ethanol
to dissolve. The heavy metal I fear most is mercury because it is
a nightmare to clean up in laboratory. Carbon black ink is the
simplest, read safest.

Wash the thinking skin with the astringent, witch hazel.
Remember that witch hazel, like cloves, contains eugenol. Air dry.
Apply vaseline and do not touch.

Poison ivy gave birth to a litter of kittens containing witch hazel
and adopted roadkill. The big cat loves milk of oats. The lion at
the door lives happily without a salivary gland and sweeps the snow
from the steps.

Witch and broom collapse to psycho-bitch, my familiar tiger
cat. My flying sofa, my tattoo to her brand, there is a trash bag of
ribbons we won in the hall closet. My baby green horse is now an
old nag and dust gathers on the medal I gave to guardian angel.

You gave me something to exchange.

Shall We Shellfish?

{sea} (too sinister)
{leveling up pollution}
-two-amino-three-
[four-[bis(two-chloroethyl)
amino] phenyl]
propanoic acid {fin}

contaminated
with chemical therapy
we were meant to treat
multiple myeloma
repeat it repeat
multiple myeloma

Hag Gift

related to witch
cut and dried for use as fuel
peat to jet lignite
if habit through habitat
angel and monster
accumulate sphagnum moss
so we are ugly
bryophytes from oyster green

so we are ugly
bogs of mostly soft water
peat to jet lignite
cut and dried for use as fuel
angel and monster
bryophytes from oyster green

Fractional Distillation

pebble pebble toil
and trouble fire burn the round
bottom to bubbles

Cyclohexane and toluene are flammable. I cleaned the cauldrons
and round bottoms and steel wool stuffed columns. Bumping into
her at her other office, she asked me how I was; and I said wanting
more fifty milliliter round bottom flasks actually. The good vulture
was afraid to order glassware.

How many round bottoms are broken the first week of organic
chemistry laboratory? (I cried because I broke one.) What is
unknown is the percent composition of your sample mixture. Is it
more fox or more hedgehog? Theory of fractional distillation helps.
I mixed the student's unknown samples; cyclohexane and toluene
are quite miscible. Boiling, like all phase changes, is an equilibrium
process represented by either a double-ended arrow or two half
arrows: one facing the past and one facing the future.

Labrador Tea

her diarrhea
derives ericaceae
her inflorescence
white umbel-like terminal
related to gate
petiolate and leather
latifolium
leaf after leaf after leaf
if thin then foil
flattened silver or wood flap
her rhododendron
northern to western to wild
rosemary to marsh
to heath brown-red underneath

Shall We Shellfish?

terminal moraine
is sills as the marking point
deposit sings heaps
creating the drumlin field
hills by the hundreds
finding the half buried egg

signal word danger
{a mean salt remembering
yellow blisters two
colors} two-chloro-N-(two-
chloroethyl)-N-
{name}methylethanamine

To Be K2-18b

a going away
kayak to eighteen bonnets
the ocean planet
hospital like telescopes
(not mini neptune)
my gift from the science gods
said home in on home
on migraine on migraine on
vanilla london
my gift from the arts gods said
or or or the rain
meaning through the looking glass
the black rabbit dance
here the presence of gases
from organisms

Rottweiler Dreams

thrice and once the hedge-
pig whined time tis time fire burn
and cauldron bubble

Capecitabine is metabolized into 5-fluorouracil, and 5-fluorouracil
is metabolized into 5-fluorouridine triphosphate and 5-fluoro-2-
deoxyuridine monophosphate. Thrice and once it read copy instead
of cape. 5-fluorouridine triphosphate competes with uridine
triphosphate for incorporation into ribonucleic acid strands.
Translate it read cut instead of cite. 5-fluoro-2-deoxyuridine
monophosphate reduces thymidine production, reducing
deoxyribonucleic acid synthesis and cell division. Binding it read
been instead of bin. My former teacher hands me the laboratory
manual: the word capecitabine was written, well, the consonants
were all there, the vowels were all wrong, but I still knew it read
capecitabine. Repeat witch and bitch; read I instead.

High Bid

old insulation
related to the hew witch
also to lay flat
the tall grass is as grass does
and over-seeding
row wind to row to row wind
listening is mine
horse to horse to horse to horse
this inheritance
bale to bale to bale to bale
ryegrass is to rye
as loose grass hay is to straw
related to air
related to the straw witch

Future Ekphrastic

double double oil
of cloves, if troubles burn and
bring cauldron bubbles

Witch hazel, also known as winter bloom to wash fresh the second
mark. Needle just below the heart, this work of art imitates what
was lost. Health allows the illusions of some humans about nudity
and pornography to continue. Illness is always rude. The once and
future witch's eyes caressing herself in the mirror, being the rest.

Bring together a surgeon and an artist, not a surgeon as an artist.
Neither a miniature pancake, nor a two pence coin, this work of
art imitates what was lost. To rest, do return, discontent without
nipples and areoles. This is some serious self-play. Re: turning and
corn muffins, what lives in the corner of her eye for everyday after
words.

Bring me a witch in the winter-time to boil cinnamon, cloves, and
nutmeg together. Bring me labradorite when I am living abroad.
Bring me restful things.

Bag Gift

basil lemon balm
lavender and dead nettles
in mint condition
the kitchen nocturnal like
pink inflorescence
a terminal hemisphere
lamiaceae
plants in the mint family
if velvet slippers
ovate lanceolate leaves
dancing princesses
in the money condition
to personify
pink wishes inflorescence

Wayward

into the cauldron
fillet of a fenny snake
medicinalis
if fens to mean eastern lands
my gift from the science gods

Utter[1]

soil or kyle
a fold of highland cattle
to pasture grasses
lactating not lactating
estrogen to make
known to give currency to
icons or coins
black ginger red and silver
a longer lifespan
than her dossan and udders
old animal legs
and horns for digging through snow
through the wild dry and
through the ground the greens buried

1   Scottish surgeon George Beatson learned from the shepherds in the Scottish highlands that the removal of the ovaries from cows altered their ability to lactate and changed the quality of their udders. This inspired oncologists to consider the role of sex hormones in the growth of breast and prostate cancers according to Siddhartha Mukherjee in *The Emperor of All Maladies*.

The Macbeth Protocol

Erinaceinae
thrice and once the urchin-pig
whined not mine, not mine
the scent past tense the first witch
needs under the hedge
sleeping through and through thunder

the familiar
hedge-pig will poison her own
keratin needles
she will anoint the unknown
once and future scent
the froth comes from her mouth from

the experiment
in the cauldron pure and cold
in all alcohol
floats and floats and floats and floats
one ingredient
dissolves and dissolving clean

is the land urchin
to hibernate through and through
her discovery
saves her witch, her coven, and
yields paclitaxel
bark of yew tree chewed and chewed

Shall We Shellfish?

mare and foliage
suffer the butterfly white
to cream horseradish
palomino pale oil
one-chloro-two-(two-
chloroethylsulfanyl)
ethane propane bute-
to tame misty and stormy

free of grit they fought
for their negligible beards
while shallots lick leeks
and garlic and shallots and
dijon and grain seeds
dissolve into sauvignon
blank the cantaloupe
as flesh so fishes its wish

October

freckles freckles toil
and trouble fire burns to ground
needle the rubble

Her spectacle that I can watch because I am not her daughter,
she is not ever, remember, burdening me. She carries me across.
This witch is a woman, a mother, and sometimes a bitch. I am
the witch's assistant. The difference between breasts and udders
is history of art and martyrs; she fights so much smarter than
that. Woman with an itch. Her breasts were the familiar beauty
of Thursdays. I know her by these four names: guardian angel,
hedgehog, toluene (which is known as methylbenzene now), witch.
Simply distill to get oil of cloves. She told me recipes, spells, total
syntheses of hexaphenylbenzene. Once upon a time, witches were
just the teachers of women, not their mothers. The freckles that
covered the round of her breasts like vinca alkaloids. The big hills
shriveled with so much mining. They feel like boiling stones. Call
them Marilyns or cupcakes, they are full of carbon and holes.
Written on the soil. Why is the measure of love the loss of cairns
and soil samples? She draws on her body circles of ball point pen,
marking rash and reaction. She would gladly again, calculate the
percentage of fluid in her lungs to the last significant figure as she
was drowning.

Next

cartilaginous
nearly identical sharks
if drifting to hide
carpets zebras whales all mine!
without otoliths
sister rays and extinct fish
fanning the nurses
through and through the twelve-week shark

the bottle kitten
silver and holding this shape
its head dorsal light
ear and ear triangles gleam
if fine cartilage
through the kittens and the sharks

Acknowledgements

I would like to thank the editors of *Poetry Wales*, *The Knicknackery*, *The Interpreter's House*, and *14 Magazine* for publishing poems from this collection.

I would like to thank *Gang Press* for publishing *NAG* as a pamphlet with original artwork in 2019.

LAY OUT YOUR UNREST

www.ingramcontent.com/pod-product-compliance
Lightning Source LLC
Chambersburg PA
CBHW051740040426
42447CB00008B/1234